ELLIS ISLAND
Doorway to Freedom

STEVEN KROLL
ILLUSTRATED BY KAREN RITZ

Holiday House/New York

Detail of column from
main building

AUTHOR'S NOTE

The "quota system," limiting immigrants by the countries they came from, was finally abolished in 1965, but the question of who should be allowed into America remains as important now as it was in the heyday of Ellis Island. With each new generation, the meaning of coming here changes. Can those of us who take America for granted willingly exclude others? There are no easy answers, but we should all be thinking about them.

For his help and boundless knowledge of Ellis Island, I would like to thank Jeffrey S. Dosik, Librarian Technician, Statue of Liberty/Ellis Island National Monument, Liberty Island, New York.

ILLUSTRATOR'S NOTE

My great-great-grandparents came to America separately from Ireland in 1873 and were processed through what was then Castle Garden. They settled in Kinderhook, New York. In those days, images of America were rendered as engravings for newspapers and other printed materials. I used pen and ink for the drawings of the early history of Ellis Island in order to capture the look of those engravings. I found pictures of immigrants and the immigration process in the library at the museum on Ellis Island. Photographs from the time period are compelling, but inconsistent, so I redrew some and created other images in pencil and watercolor.

Text copyright © 1995 by Steven Kroll
Illustrations copyright © 1995 by Karen Ritz
All rights reserved
Printed in the United States of America
First Edition

Library of Congress Cataloging-in-Publication Data
Kroll, Steven.
Ellis Island : doorway to freedom / Steven Kroll ; illustrated by
Karen Ritz. — 1st ed.
p.   cm.
Summary: Describes how the immigration station on Ellis Island
served as a gateway into the United States for more than sixteen
million immigrants between 1892 and 1954.
ISBN 0-8234-1192-3
1. United States—Emigration and immigration—Juvenile literature.
2. Ellis Island Immigration Station (New York, N.Y.)—History—
Juvenile literature.   [1. United States—Emigration and
immigration.   2. Ellis Island Immigration Station (New York, N.Y.)—
History.]   I. Ritz, Karen, ill.   II. Title.
JV6450.K76   1995   95-714   CIP   AC
325.73—dc20

NEW YORK HARBOR

Ellis Island

Bedlow's Island
(Liberty Island)

New Jersey

Ellis Island lies in Upper New York Bay, directly across from the island of Manhattan. It covers twenty-seven-and-a-half acres and has thirty-six buildings. Between 1892 and 1954, more than sixteen million people passed through its doors, hoping to become Americans.

Before landfill made the island larger, it was only three-and-a-half acres. In the 1600s, it was owned first by the Dutch, then by the British, as they came to the shores of America. By 1780, the island belonged to the American merchant Samuel Ellis. He built a tavern there, but in 1794, the United States was getting close to war with Great Britain. New York State began building forts around New York Harbor. Ellis Island was chosen as one of the sites.

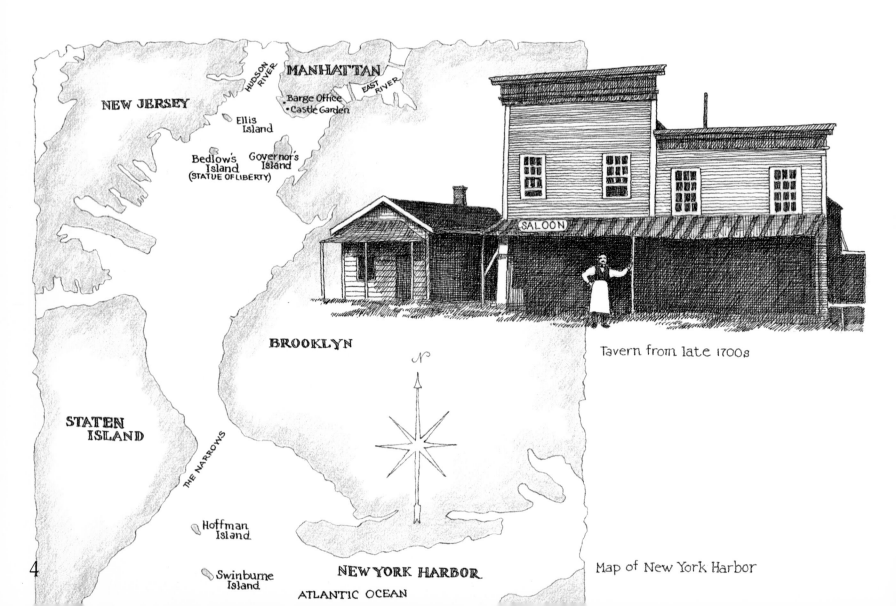

Tavern from late 1700s

Map of New York Harbor

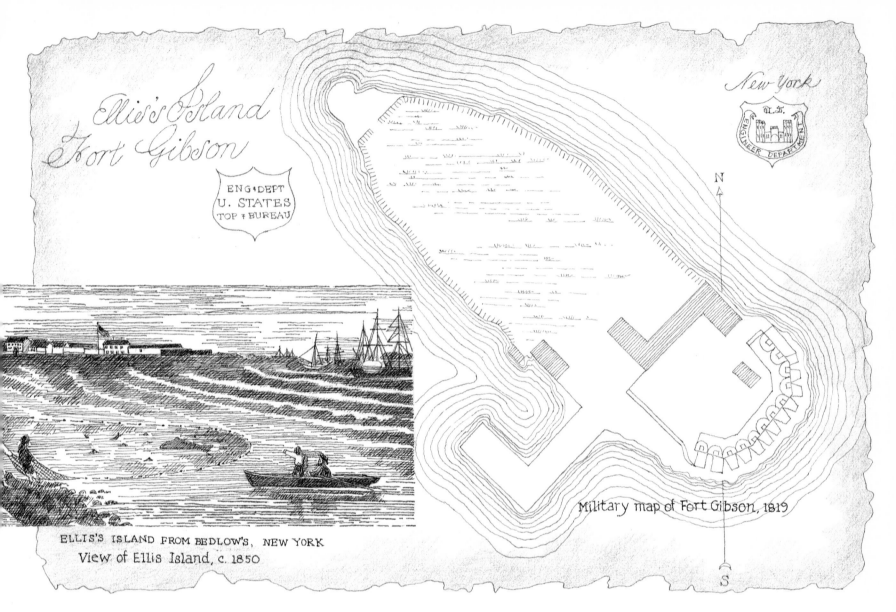

Ellis's Island
Fort Gibson

ENG·DEPT
U. STATES
TOP·BUREAU

New York

N

ELLIS'S ISLAND FROM BEDLOW'S, NEW YORK
View of Ellis Island, c. 1850

Military map of Fort Gibson, 1819

S

Progress was slow. In 1808 New York State bought the island from the Ellis family and gave it to the federal government. The government wanted to make sure the forts were completed before war came, and they were—just in time for the War of 1812. But it was all for nothing. The forts weren't involved in the fighting, and afterwards, Fort Gibson on Ellis Island became a place for the U.S. Navy to store ammunition.

Meanwhile, thousands of people were coming to America in search of a better life. They arrived at ports in Boston, San Francisco, and New Orleans, but mostly they arrived in New York. Between 1848 and 1854, Germans, French, and Irish crowded the New York City docks. Often they were robbed and cheated. The State decided it would be safer and easier for immigrants to pass through the old Southwest Battery fort at the tip of Manhattan. By then, the fort had become a concert hall named Castle Garden.

Italian immigrant child

6

As early as 1882, immigrants from southern and eastern Europe outnumbered those from northern and western Europe. Southern Italians, Greeks, Poles, Austro-Hungarians, Russians, and Eastern European Jews swelled to a flood between 1892 and 1914.

With so many people coming to America, the U.S. government found it necessary to take control of immigration in 1890. At the Port of New York, Castle Garden had become too small, and people were still getting robbed and cheated.

Hungarian immigrant family

7

The government chose Ellis Island to replace Castle Garden. At the same time the navy's ammunition was shifted from the island to Fort Wadsworth on the Narrows.

The new immigration station took two years to build. During that time, immigrants passed through the Barge Office, a cramped U.S. Customs Service building not far from Castle Garden.

Constucting the immigration station

Barge office

Dutch immigrant children

8

First Ellis Island immigration station

Statue of Annie Moore, Ellis Island.

ANNIE MOORE
FIRST IMMIGRANT PROCESSED AT ELLIS ISLAND
JANUARY 1, 1892

UNVEILED BY
THE PRESIDENT OF IRELAND
MARY ROBINSON

A GIFT TO
THE PEOPLE OF THE UNITED STATES OF AMERICA
FROM THE IRISH AMERICAN CULTURAL INSTITUTE
JOHN P. WALSH, CHAIRMAN
MAY 18, 1993
SCULPTOR: JEANNE RYNHART, COUNTY CORK

The Ellis Island Immigration Station opened on January 1, 1892. The island had been doubled in size with landfill. In front of the big main building, a channel had been dug deep enough for ferries to dock. Other buildings contained a hospital, a dormitory, and a kitchen.

9

Between 1892 and 1897, one million five hundred thousand immigrants passed through the new immigration buildings. On June 15, 1897, a mysterious fire burned the entire wooden station to the ground. Immigrants returned to the Barge Office while another station was built.

Immigrant children

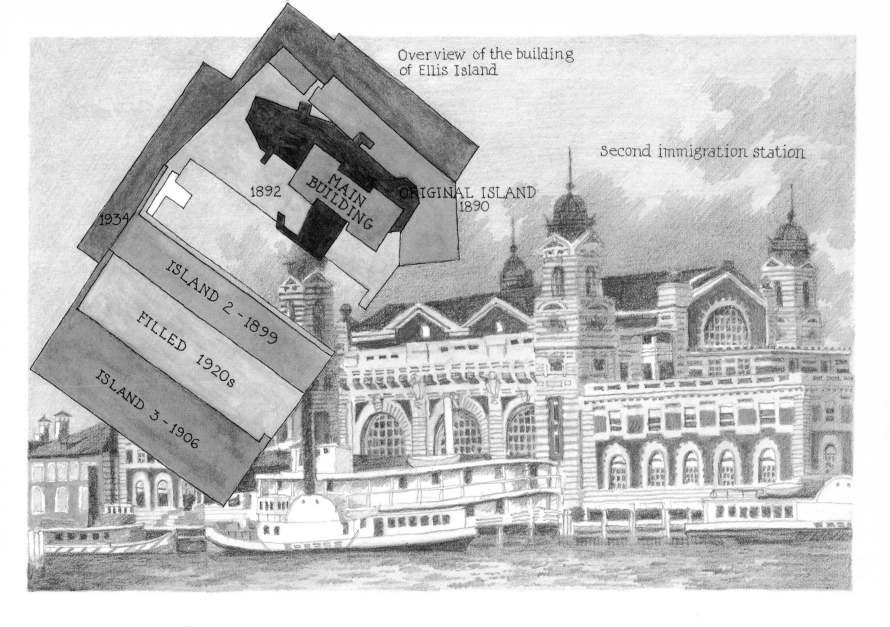

Overview of the building
of Ellis Island

Second immigration station

1892

MAIN
BUILDING

ORIGINAL ISLAND
1890

1934

ISLAND 2 - 1899

FILLED 1920s

ISLAND 3 - 1906

The second immigration station on Ellis Island opened December 17, 1900. There was another large main building, as well as a kitchen, a laundry, and a bathhouse. Landfill had created a second island linked to the first. A hospital opened there in 1902. On a third island, also made of landfill, another hospital was completed in 1910. It was for people who had tuberculosis and other contagious diseases.

All the buildings were fireproof. The main building, with its red brick, limestone trim, and four domed towers, looked like a palace.

The immigrants kept pouring in. Before arrival, most of them had been jammed together for a week to a month on the lower deck of a steamship. This was the cheapest way to travel and was called steerage.

Sailing posters

Steerage passengers

13

When the ship steamed into Lower New York Bay, doctors checked all passengers for serious diseases that might spread, like smallpox and typhus. Those infected were taken to Swinburne Island. Those exposed but not infected went to Hoffman Island for observation.

Going through the Narrows, the doctors gave first and second class passengers a more thorough exam. Almost all received permission to land. When the ship reached the Hudson River piers, only the steerage passengers were left to be ferried to Ellis Island.

Postcards of steamships

15

Ellis Island ferry

With so many arrivals, the wait to get on a ferry could last for days. The ferries themselves were packed and had no decent toilets. The short ride to the island could take hours as delay followed delay.

Baggage room

Once the immigrants had landed on Ellis Island, they hurried inside the main building. Some left their luggage in the first floor baggage room. Others, warned about robberies, carried everything with them.

17

B Back   H Heart   Pg Pregnancy

C Conjunctivitis   L Lameness

Room of men suspected of mental illness

E Eyes   N Neck   S Senility

Ft Feet   P Physical and lungs   X Suspected mental illness

Clambering up the stairs, the immigrants were watched by doctors. Anyone who seemed to have something wrong had his coat marked with chalk: L for lameness, H for heart disease, X for a possible mental problem. These people were taken aside and given more thorough exams upstairs.

Everyone else entered the huge Registry Room, or Great Hall. Iron pipe railings divided twelve narrow aisles, though in 1911, the railings were replaced by benches. It was very noisy.

Great Hall

Scottish immigrant children

19

Buttonhook

The immigrants inched down the aisles. A doctor examined them in what was called "the six-second medical." There was also an eye exam, and it was the most feared. Looking for trachoma, an eye disease that could cause blindness, the doctors rolled back the inner eyelid. Usually they did it with a buttonhook.

After the medical examinations, most reached the immigration inspectors at the other end of the room. Flanked by interpreters, the inspectors asked the immigrants questions: What's your name? Are you married? How will you make a living in America?

Immigrants from the West Indies

U. S. immigration inspector's hat

21

Almost all answered well enough to be given a landing card. These immigrants could then exchange their foreign money for American dollars and buy railroad tickets or, perhaps, a snack from the Ellis Island food service. Train travelers were ferried to terminals in Jersey City or Hoboken. The rest walked through a door marked "Push. To New York." Friends and relatives were waiting at the "Kissing Post of America," and so was a ferry to Manhattan.

- card
- exchange money

MONEY EXCHANGE

Foreign currency

Place setting from Ellis Island food service

Hospital beds

Those kept back slept in a dormitory. They might be waiting to have a sick child released from the hospital or to defend their rights—to show they were not criminals; to argue that they could support their families—before a group of examiners. Only two out of every hundred immigrants were eventually returned to the lands they had come from.

By the 1880s, Americans were complaining that immigrants were taking their jobs. The Chinese had helped build the railroads, and some American workers were angry that they accepted lower wages. In 1882, the first of several laws was passed to keep the Chinese out. Because many Americans didn't want the government to have to support those immigrants who could not support themselves, a law was also passed to keep out anyone "liable to become a public charge." To try to keep immigrants from taking jobs from those already here, the Contract Labor Act of 1885 prevented anyone from entering America who already had a "contract for work."

Sheet music

Chinese store owner

When World War I began in 1914, immigration slowed. In spite of that, Congress passed the Literacy Act of 1917, requiring any immigrant over the age of sixteen to read a forty-word passage in his native language.

America entered the war that April. Ellis Island was used to hold foreigners suspected of siding with the German enemy. It also held the crews from some German merchant ships. When the war ended in 1918, the army and the navy used the island for treating sick and wounded servicemen.

German prisoners

Great Hall during World War II

Great Hall in later years

MODERN
BOSTON TEA PARTY
NO REDS
WANTED

Angry outbursts against foreigners after the war led to the "Red Scare" of 1919–1920. Hundreds of Communists and others who spoke out against the U.S. government were brought to Ellis Island. Many were forced to leave the country.

The island was opened again to inspect immigrants in 1920, but the feeling against foreigners, especially southern and eastern Europeans, was still strong. In 1921 and 1924, Congress passed acts limiting the number of immigrants from all countries, but especially from those that were unpopular. The Immigration Act of 1924 also made it possible for immigrants to be examined before they left for America.

Eastern European immigrants being questioned by an interpreter-stenographer team

Now Ellis Island was no longer needed as an immigration station. It became a center for holding suspicious foreigners, as well as a place to receive people escaping from Hitler's Germany. During World II it was a Coast Guard station. In November 1954, it closed.

President Lyndon Johnson made Ellis Island part of the Statue of Liberty National Monument in 1965. In 1982 the Statue of Liberty/Ellis Island Foundation was set up to restore both monuments. After a lot of work, the entire main building was returned to the way it looked between 1918 and 1924. Its three floors were filled with exhibits telling the story of American immigration. In September 1990, the Ellis Island Immigration Museum opened to the public, a fitting reminder that in America we are all immigrants.

GLOSSARY

buttonhook: a small hook, usually metal and with a short handle, for pulling buttons through buttonholes.

Coast Guard: a branch of the United States military service that enforces laws and helps people at sea.

Congress: the law-making branch of the United States government, divided into two separate groups: the Senate and the House of Representatives.

contagious disease: a disease easily spread from one person to another.

Customs Service: the branch of the Department of the Treasury that collects taxes on goods brought into the country and enforces laws to do with smuggling.

immigrant: a person who leaves his country for another, usually intending to stay there.

interpreter: someone who translates the words of one language into the words of another language, in this case English.

landfill: trash and garbage used in layers covered by soil to make an area larger.

The Narrows: the thin strip where Lower New York Bay passes between Staten Island and Brooklyn and becomes Upper New York Bay.

smallpox: a contagious disease, caused by a virus and identified by blisters on the skin.

Statue of Liberty: a statue of a woman holding a burning torch that stands on Liberty Island in New York Harbor. It was designed by Frédéric-Auguste Bartholdi and dedicated in 1886.

trachoma: a contagious eye disease that causes swellings on the inner eyelid.

tuberculosis: a contagious disease that causes small, lumplike swellings, usually in the lungs.

typhus: a disease, passed on by lice and fleas, that causes exhaustion, headaches, and reddish spots on the body.

War of 1812: a war between Great Britain and the United States over trade restrictions and the forced removal of American sailors from their ships that lasted from 1812 to 1815.

World War I: a huge war, fought between 1914 and 1918, and involving the Central Powers (Germany and Austria-Hungary) against the Allies (Great Britain, France, Russia, the United States, and others), with the Allies finally winning.

World War II: an even huger war, fought between 1939 and 1945, and involving the Axis (Germany, Italy, and Japan) against the Allies (Great Britain, France, the United States from 1941, and many others), with the Allies winning once again.

INDEX